MW00879366

Easy 5 Ing.
Cooker Cookbook

Quick And Easy 5 Ingredient Crock Pot Recipes

Karen Ellgen

TERMS & CONDITIONS

TABLE OF CONTENTS

Chapter 1: The Many Advantages of Healthy Crock Pot Cooking

Healthy crock pot cooking allows families to prepare their meals, have it cooked & be ready at dinner time with a lot less effort. Once all the simple ingredients have been combined into a slow cooker (crock pot) you may easily set the meal to cook properly while away at work, or out enjoying other activities. In fact,the foods cooked in a slow cooker/ crock pot tend to have more intense & amazing flavors because of the extended cooking time. Having the amazing ability to control all added ingredients may easily enhance the nutrient content of every family meal.

The 1st slow cooking crock pot was manufactured in the early 1970s. As the time passes, by the end of that decade, companies had made them easier to clean. Within the 1st few years, hundreds of fantastic quality cookbooks dedicated to slow cooking became very popular with the home chefs.

Increased Nutrient Content

During any cooking process, there tends to be a breakdown & nutrients, with the exception of lycopene that often is heightened during cooking. Fortunately, a crock pot offer significant benefits over other cooking methods because of its relatively low heat an extended cooking time. The lower temperature tends not to destroy healthy nutrients, which is often the downside to boiling or steaming.

Recapturing juices & sauces with the slow cooker tends to increase the results of healthy crock pot cooking.

Reduced Processed Food Consumption

One of the greatest advantages of a slow cooker is the ability to reduce the consumption of harmful processed foods. In fact, a slow cooker provides the opportunity to decrease the amount of sodium intake, while reducing calories & fat in the family's diet. Prepackaged meals purchased from the frozen or box section of the store may now be easily prepared using the family's slow cooker. As an example, the home chef may find a wide assortment of recipes specifically designed for the slow cooker including soups, casseroles, roasts & even baked desserts.

Aside from healthy crock pot cooking results, there are other significant advantages to using a slow cooker. These include:

• A Timesaver - A lot of meals prepared in the slow cooker require only the single pot. There is only minimal initial preparation required, & the slow cooker will perform all the work while the family is away.

• Reduced Energy Consumption - Slow cookers are manufactured to use substantially less electricity than through conventional ovens & stoves.

• Simply Cleanup - Manufacturers now create crock pots that are simply to clean. The pot basically lifts out of the cooker & may be placed in the dishwasher, or cleaned at the sink. With the exception of cutting utensils & a cutting board, all meals are prepared in the crock pot.

• Useful during Every Season - Because the slow cooker doesn't emit high levels of heat inside the kitchen, it works well for year-round cooking. There is a huge wide range of recipes available including comfort foods for the wintertime, & simply to repair meals for the summer.

With the amazing ability to use less expensive meats, cooking at lower temperatures & also controlling nutrient content, preparing meals in a slow cooker makes sense. It offers convenience, because it cooks the meals while the chef is away.

Nutritious Meals

Having the ability to control every meal's nutrient profile helps maintain a healthy family. As an e.g., adding organic vegetables to a recipe helps increase the nutrient content of the meal while adding more bulk & fiber from the vegetables. In fact, high-quality tougher cuts of meat turn out perfectly when the cooking time is extended at a lower temperature. Often times, these meats become fork tender without the need to add tenderizers or fat. This helps the family maintain a lower calorie content & consume leaner cuts.

Chapter 2: Choosing the Right Slow Cooker

There are a few things you need to consider when choosing the right slow cooker. The guideline below will help you pick the right slow cooker that meets all your cooking needs.

1. Heating

This is something that you need to ask to the salesperson at the shop where you're buying the slow cooker. A lot of slow cookers have the heating mechanism at the bottom of cooker, while others have heating not only at the bottom but also along the sides. You might want to choose the second type that heats at the bottom & sides because this means that heat is evenly distributed throughout the pot, which allows the food to cook evenly.

2. The pot or crock

The pot itself may be made in different ceramic, porcelain, namely, materials, & metal. The most common materials used for making the crock are porcelain & ceramic. Only a few are made of metal because they're heavier. All of these materials work well & are great conductors of heat. The most crucial thing is that they're removable so that you may clean them when they get dirty. It also just boils down to your preference, whether you like porcelain, ceramic, or metal.

3. Shape

Slow cookers only come in 2 shapes-- round or oval. Choosing which 1 is the main is based more on what you're planning to cook mostly in the crock pot. For instance, if you're planning to cook ribs, brisket, or whole chicken, then you might want to choose oval shaped slow cookers. If you're going to cook mainly stews & soups, then any shape is okay. You might also want to consider where you're planning to put or store the slow cooker. Oval slow cookers might occupy too much space on your tiny counter, or round slow cookers might not fit in your short kitchen cabinet.

4. The lid or cover

For slow cookers, the lid serves a more crucial purpose than basically covering the food. It also keeps the heat from escaping the pot, which helps cook the food faster. The most popular lids are made of glass because they're heavy, which seals the pot perfectly, & they're see-through, which allows you to check on whatever your cooking without lifting the lid. Try to avoid choosing slow cooker with a lid made of plastic or other light & opaque materials.

5. Timer

If you're the type of customer who always need reminders to not forget crucial things, then you need to consider buying a slow cooker with a built in timer. You may set the timer depending on how long you need to cook the dish, which you may find in the recipe. By setting the time built in at the slow cooker, you're making sure that the food that you're cooking won't be scorched or won't turn to mush because you completely forgot all about it.

6. Size

The size of the slow cooker is another crucial consideration. If you live alone & you just need to cook for yourself, a tiny slow cooker is ideal for you. A lot of people who have a small family also opt for these small three to four quart slow cookers because they do not want any leftovers. There are also small slow cookers that are used for keeping dips & sauces warm during special gatherings. But if you're just starting, it's main to get yourself an average-sized cooker because a lot of recipes are made for these slow cookers & you might find it difficult to scale down the recipe particularly if this is your 1st time to use a slow cooker. The average size is about six quarts. But if you've a large family or maybe if you love parties & get togethers & you're confident cooking for a large group of people, then you may choose something bigger.

7. Searing feature

More expensive models of slow cookers come with a searing function which lets you sautée vegetables or onions & brown meats. Searing is a process of cooking that caramelize the food & release its flavor. A lot of slow cookers allow you to sear on the pot itself before you change the setting to 'slow cook' while others have a pot that you may put over your stove for searing ingredients. Either way, you're still just using one vessel. Keep in mind though that pans are usually wider than a crock pot & searing requires you to toss the ingredients around the pan to cook them properly. If you think it will be difficult for you to sear in the pot insert or if you're in a budget & don't really mind using the stove & another pan for searing, then just buy a main slow cooker that does not have this additional function.

8. Warming feature

A lot of slow cookers have temperature settings at high & low. There are also a lot of which have the warming function, which allows you to keep the food warm at a low temperature without further cooking the food. You may choose 1 that has a warming function tied in with the timer. This means that the crock pot will automatically change its setting to warm function after the timer goes off. This is a great feature if you're planning to use your slow cooker in potlucks or maybe special gatherings where you want to serve warm food.

9. Price

Of course, the price tag is another crucial consideration particularly if your budget is limited. Small slow cookers are usually cheaper than bigger ones. Extra features may also make the slow cooker more expensive. The brand of the slow cooker also affects the price. However, buying from known brands that everyone knows provide high quality kitchen appliances is something that you should do even if they will cost you a little more money. In the long run, it will save you more money because your slow cooker will last for a long time & you won't need to spend a lot of money on repairs.

Simply, the things that you need to consider when buying a slow cooker depend a lot on your needs, preferences, & budget. You might want to read reviews & ratings of different slow cookers from different review websites to help you make a decision on which slow cooker to buy.

It's also crucial to learn a lot of useful tips & tricks for slow cooking that will help you cook the perfect meals for you & your family.

Chapter 3: Recipes

Now go ahead and check out these amazing 5 ingredient slow cooker recipes.

Titanic Spinach-Tomato Casserole (Slow Cooked)

Different take on this one...

Ingredients:

- 1/2 cup milk
- About 3/4 cup feta cheese
- 1/2 cup sun-dried tomatoes
- 2 cups spinach
- 12 eggs

Instructions:

1. First of all, please make sure you've all the ingredients available. Whisk eggs & milk together.
2. Now mix in the tomatoes & spinach.
3. Grease your Crock-Pot & then pour in the egg mixture.
4. Then top with feta cheese & close the lid.
5. One thing remains to be done. Cook properly on LOW for about 4 to 6 hours.
6. Finally serve!

Serves: 4 to 6

Prep time: About 5 to 10 minutes

Cooking time: 4 to 6 hours

I can eat them all day!!

Nutritional Information:

Total calories: 420

Protein: 35

Carbs: 8

Fat: 27

Fiber: 1

Tasty Mighty Bacon and Egg Casserole

Wow, just wow!!

Ingredients:

- 1 bell pepper (Diced)
- Cooking Spray
- About 1.5 onion (Chopped)
- 12 eggs
- Salt and ground black pepper
- 1 cup whole milk
- About 8.5 slices pre-cooked bacon

Directions:

1. First of all, please make sure you've all the ingredients available. Quickly spray the inside of the pot with cooking spray.
2. Now quickly whisk eggs, milk, salt & pepper in a bowl.
3. This step is important. Cook properly the onion and bell pepper in a skillet

over medium heat until softened and fragrant, about 2 to 5 minutes.

4. Remove from heat, & let cool down for a few minutes.
5. Then add bell pepper, onion, and bacon to the egg mixture.
6. One thing remains to be done. Please pour the egg mixture into the slow cooker.
7. Finally cook properly on LOW for about 6 to 8 hours, until the eggs are set and cooked.

Serves: 6 to 8

Preparation time: 15 to 20 minutes

Cooking time: 6 hours on LOW

Show time!!

Nutritional information:

Carbs 13.5 g

Protein 157 g

Sodium 1489 mg

Calories 565

Fat 132 g

Yummy Tasty Ricotta and Spinach Egg Casserole

Supreme level.

Ingredients:

- Cooking spray
- 1/4 cup heavy whipping cream
- 12 large eggs
- About 1.5 cup ricotta cheese
- 1 small yellow onion (Diced)
- 9-ounce box frozen spinach, water squeezed out
- About 1/2 teaspoon salt

Directions:

1. First of all, please make sure you've all the ingredients available. Now quickly grease sides & bottom of Slow Cooker with cooking spray.

2. Now in a blender, blend until smooth the ricotta cheese, onion, whipping cream & 4 eggs.

3. This step is important. Once smooth, set aside.

4. In a bowl, whisk well remaining eggs.

5. Then season with salt & whisk well.

6. Stir in blended mixture & mix again.

7. Add spinach and mix well.

8. One thing remains to be done. Pour into slow cooker.

9. Finally cover & cook properly on low for about 6 to 7 hours or on high for about 3 to 4 hours.

Serves: 6 to 7

Cooking Time: 7 hours

Preparation Time: 10 to 15 minutes

Sincere efforts will be awesome.

Nutritional information:

Protein: 10.26g

Fiber: 0.1g

Fat: 17.02

Carbohydrates: 3.18g

Sodium: 152mg

Sugar: 0.75g

Calories per serving: 209

Unique Mighty Tasty Strawberry Rhubarb Jam

This is different, isn't it?

Ingredients:

- 2 pounds rhubarb (Chopped)
- About 1 teaspoon cinnamon
- 1 cup of sugar
- 3 pounds fresh strawberries (Chopped)

Directions:

1. First of all, please make sure you've all the ingredients available. Layer half the strawberry & rhubarb in the slow cooker.
2. Now sprinkle half cup of sugar over the fruit.
3. Place the rest of the strawberries & rhubarb on the sugar.

4.   This step is important. Sprinkle evenly the remaining sugar & the cinnamon powder on top.

5.   Cover and cook properly for about 3 to 4 hours on LOW.

6.   Then remove the lid, stir the jam & cook further for about 1.5 hour on LOW with the lid off. Continue cooking until you get your desired consistency.

7.   One thing remains to be done. Mash the jam for chunky consistency, or use a blender for a smooth jam.

8.   Finally serve this yummy jam on toast or with vanilla ice cream, yogurt, or pancakes.

Serves: 30 to 32

Preparation time: 20 to 25 minutes

Cooking time: 7 hours on LOW

Yeah, this is a new variation.

Nutritional information:

Protein 0 g

Fat 1.9 g

Calories 55

Carbs 14 g

Ultimate Feta-Kale Egg Casserole

Be unique, be extraordinary...

Ingredients:

- 5-ounce baby kale
- 1 cup low-fat sour cream
- 1/4 cup sliced green onion
- 8 eggs
- 5-ounce crumbled Feta cheese
- Salt and pepper to taste

Directions:

1. First of all, please make sure you've all the ingredients available. Grease sides & bottom of Slow Cooker with cooking spray.
2. Then place a nonstick skillet on medium high fire & grease with cooking spray.

3.	Sauté kale until it is flat and softened, around 2 to 5 minutes.
4.	Now in a large bowl, beat eggs & season with pepper and salt.
5.	Mix in kale, green onion and feta cheese.
6.	One thing remains to be done. Pour into pot, cover, & cook properly on low for about 2 to 3 hours.
7.	Finally to serve, place a dollop of sour cream on top of a slice of the dish.

Serves: 6 to 7

Cooking Time: 3 hours 4 minutes

Preparation Time: 15 to 20 minutes

Something is special!!

Nutritional information:

Carbohydrates: 8.54g

Fiber: 1g

Protein: 19.64g

Sodium: mg

Fat: 24.25g

Sugar: 5.2g

Calories per serving: 334

Iconic Breakfast Piquant Eggs (Crock Pot)

If you're a legend, then make this one.

Ingredients:

- 2 green onion sliced
- Salt to taste
- 2 pinch grated hot pepper (or to taste)
- 8 eggs
- About 1.5 tsp cumin
- 2 Tbps of olive oil

Directions:

1. First of all, please make sure you've all the ingredients available. Now quickly heat the olive oil in a frying pan & then sauté the green onions for about 2 to 3 minutes.
2. Now season salt, hot pepper, & the cumin.
3. This step is important. Transfer the onion to your greased Crock Pot.

4. Now quickly whisk the eggs with a pinch of salt & the extra hot pepper if needed.

5. Then pour the egg mixture over the green onions in your Crock Pot.

6. One thing remains to be done. Cover and cook properly on HIGH for about 2.5 hours.

7. Finally sprinkle with chopped parsley or dill and serve hot.

Servings: 4 to 5

Cooking Times

Total Time: 2 hours & 10 to 15 minutes

Being lucky is definitely better.

Nutritional information:

Sodium 145,54mg 6%

Total Fat 16,45g 25%

Saturated Fat 4,1g 21%

Calories 230,09

Sugar 2,98g

Protein 13,37g 27%

Calories From Fat (64%) 146,94

% Daily Value

Cholesterol 372mg 124%

Potassium 242,01mg 7%

Total Carbohydrates 6,92g 2%

Fiber 1,2g 5%

Awesome Healthy Sausage and Beans Recipe

If you're a legend, then make this one.

Ingredients:

- 1 (25-ounce) jar tomatoes, crushed
- Water
- About 1.5 tablespoon garlic powder (or more)
- 12 ounces kielbasa sausage
- About 1.5 tablespoon Celtic sea salt (or more)
- 4 cups white beans

Directions:

1. First of all, please make sure you've all the ingredients available. Steep the beans in water overnight, at room temperature.

2.	Now drain the beans & place them in your crockpot.

3.	Now quickly add enough water to cover the beans & then throw in the rest of the ingredients.

4.	Then cook everything on HIGH for about 7 to 8 hours.

5.	One thing remains to be done. Adjust the salt & garlic powder as needed.

6.	Finally transfer the dish to a bowl & serve.

Serves: 8 – Prep.

Time: 10 to 15 minutes

Cooking Time: 8 hours

Nutritional information:

Sodium 776 mg

Total Fat 25 g

Protein 20 g

Calories 422

Carbs 27 g

Being lucky is definitely better.

Super Vintage Bell Pepper-Broccoli Egg Casserole

Awesome, isn't it?

Ingredients:

- About 1 teaspoon pepper
- 3/4 cup milk
- 8 eggs
- 2 bell peppers, chopped roughly
- 6-ounce cheddar cheese
- About 1.5 teaspoon salt
- 1 small head of broccoli, roughly chopped

Directions:

1. First of all, please make sure you've all the ingredients available. Now please grease sides and the bottom of Slow Cooker with cooking spray.

2. Then place 1/2 of broccoli on bottom of pot, then 1/2 of bell

peppers, & then followed by 1/2 of cheese.

3.   This step is important. Repeat this process until cheese & broccoli are used up.

4.   In a bowl, whisk well eggs, pepper, salt, and milk.

5.   One thing remains to be done. Now pour egg mixture into pot.

6.   Finally cover and cook properly on low settings for about 3 to 4 hours.

Serves: 8 to 9

Cooking Time: 4 hours

Preparation Time: 15 to 20 minutes

Luxury tasty dish for you!!

Nutritional information:

Fiber: 1.3g

Protein: 13.82g

Sodium: 647mg

Carbohydrates: 7.41g

Fat: 12.41g

Sugar: 4.5g

Calories per serving: 196

Delightful Best Cream Cheese & Mushroom Egg Casserole

Get ready to make it my way!!

Ingredients:

- 12 medium eggs
- About 3/4 cup shredded Mexican blend cheese
- 1/2 cup milk
- 8-ounce fresh mushrooms, cleaned and sliced
- 8-ounce cream cheese, cut into small cubes
- Pepper and salt to taste

Directions:

1. First of all, please make sure you've all the ingredients available. Now quickly grease sides & the bottom of Slow Cooker with cooking spray.

2. Now place a nonstick skillet on medium high fire & cook mushrooms properly for about 10 to 15 minutes, until soft.

3. This step is important. Meanwhile, whisk well eggs. Season with pepper and salt.

4. Pour in milk & whisk well.

5. With a slotted spoon, transfer softened mushrooms into slow cooker & evenly spread on the bottom.

6. Then top with cream cheese.

7. Pour in egg mixture.

8. One thing remains to be done. Top with cheese.

9. Finally cover and cook properly for about 2 to 3 hours on high settings.

Serves: 8 to 9

Cooking Time: 2 hours 40 to 50 minutes

Preparation Time: 15 to 20 minutes

The best combo ever!!

Nutritional information:

Carbohydrates: 24.22g

Fiber: 3.3g

Protein: 15.26g

Sodium: 252mg

Fat: 17.17g

Sugar: 3.01g

Calories per serving: 299

Fantastic Banana and Coconut Milk Steel-Cut Oats

Mystery is unveiled!!

Ingredients:

- 2 cans coconut milk, unsweetened
- About 1 teaspoon cinnamon
- 1 cup steel cut oats
- 2 tablespoons brown sugar
- 2 medium ripe bananas (Sliced)

Directions:

1. First of all, please make sure you've all the ingredients available. Place all ingredients in the crockpot.
2. Then add a dash of salt if needed.
3. Give a good stir.
4. One thing remains to be done. Now close the lid & cook properly on low for about 2 to 3 hours.
5. Finally once cooked, serve with a tablespoon of melted butter.

Serves: 7 to 8

Preparation Time: 5 to 10 minutes

Cooking Time: 3 hours

The speed matters...

Nutritional information:

Carbohydrates: 15.3g

Fiber:2.6g

Fat: 5.9g

Calories per serving:101

Protein: 2.6g

Titanic Creamy Chicken Curry

Supreme level.

Ingredients:

- About 2.5 tablespoons curry powder
- 1/2 cup plain yogurt
- 3/4 cup water
- Salt and black pepper
- 1 medium diced onion
- 2 pounds bone-in, skinless chicken thighs
- 1/3 cup tomato paste

Directions:

1. First of all, please make sure you've all the ingredients available. Mix

together the curry powder, tomato paste, and water in the slow cooker.

2. Now add the onion & stir.
3. This step is important. Now quickly add the chicken thighs & then season with salt and pepper.
4. Cover and cook properly for about 7 to 8 hours on LOW or for about 3 to 4 hours on HIGH.
5. One thing remains to be done. Then stir in the yogurt and continue cooking for about 5 to 10 minutes on LOW.
6. Finally serve with rice & steamed vegetables.

Serves: 6 to 7

Preparation time: 15 to 20 minutes

Cooking time: 7 hours on LOW or 3 to 4 hours on HIGH

Sincere efforts will be awesome.

Nutritional information:

Sodium 521.3 mg

Fat 14.5 g

Protein 47.6 g

Calories 363.8

Carbs 8.3 g

Pinnacle Crock-Pot Cheesy Chicken

Light taste.

Ingredients:

- About 1.5 teaspoon garlic salt
- 1 cup mozzarella cheese (Shredded)
- 1 cup cream cheese
- 1 cup sugar-free tomato sauce
- 2 pounds chicken breasts

Directions:

1. First of all, please make sure you've all the ingredients available. Now season the chicken breasts with garlic salt & add to the crock pot.
2. One thing remains to be done. Then put the remaining ingredients in the pot & set the crock pot on Low.
3. Finally cook properly for about 6 to 7 hours and dish out.

Serving: 6 to 7

Preparation Time: 10 to 15 minutes

Cook Time: 7 hours 10 to 15 minutes

Legendary taste.

Nutritional information:

Calories: 238

Fat: 16.2g

Carbohydrates: 1.5g

Protein: 20.5g

Perfect Crock-Pot Chicken Wings

Oh yeah. This is the recipe I was waiting for.

Ingredients:

- 1/4 cup apple cider vinegar
- Salt and black pepper, to taste
- 1 cup Frank's red hot sauce
- About 1.5 tablespoon ghee
- 1 pound chicken wings

Directions:

1. First of all, please make sure you've all the ingredients available. Now mix together apple cider vinegar, Frank's red hot sauce, ghee, salt & black pepper in a bowl.
2. One thing remains to be done. Then put the chicken wings & sauce in the crock pot and set the crock pot on Low.
3. Finally cook properly for about 5 to 6 hours and dish out.

Serving: 3 to 4

Preparation Time: 5 to 10 minutes

Cook Time: 6 hours 15 to 20 minutes

Simplicity is best.

Nutritional information:

Calories: 332

Fat: 15.5g

Carbohydrates: 0.9g

Protein: 43.8g

Rich Citrus infused Chicken Breasts

Let's dive in…

Ingredients:

- 1 can cream of chicken soup
- Water
- Juice of half a lemon
- Cooking spray
- 2 large oranges, 1 juiced, 1 sliced
- Salt and pepper
- 4 boneless and skinless chicken breasts
- About 1.5 tablespoon of lemon pepper seasoning

Directions:

1. First of all, please make sure you've all the ingredients available. Grease the bottom of the slow cooker with cooking spray.

2. Now season the chicken breasts with salt & pepper.

3. Place the orange slices at the bottom of the slow cooker.

4. This step is important. Let the chicken breasts sit on the oranges.

5. Then pour the soup in a bowl, add lemon & orange juice and lemon pepper.

6. Add 1/2 can of water to the mix. Whisk until well combined.

7. Now pour it over the chicken in the slow cooker.

8. One thing remains to be done. Cook properly for about 2 to 3 hours on HIGH or 6 hours on LOW.

9. Finally serve with your favorite vegetables & rice.

Serves: 2 to 4

Preparation time: 10 to 15 minutes

Cooking time: 3 hours on HIGH or 6 hours on LOW

Your friends and family are waiting. Hurry!!

Nutritional information:

Carbs 34.52 g

Sodium 1809 mg

Fat 37.07 g

Protein 45.31 g

Calories 670

Elegant Lemony Chicken with Garlic

Royal taste…

Ingredients:

- All-purpose chicken seasoning
- Fresh herbs of your choice
- Salt and pepper
- 3 heads of garlic, outer peel removed
- 4 lemons
- 1 large chicken, about 4 pounds

Directions:

1. First of all, please make sure you've all the ingredients available. Rinse the chicken & pat it dry.
2. Now rub the seasonings on the outside of the chicken, & in the cavity.
3. Slice two of the lemons and garlic heads, & layer them on the bottom of the slow cooker.

4. This step is important. Sprinkle with herbs.

5. Then stuff the chicken with a garlic head & a lemon cut in quarters & lay the chicken on the lemon & garlic layer in the slow cooker.

6. Slice the remaining lemon, & arrange it over the chicken.

7. Sprinkle with herbs.

8. Now cover and cook properly for about 3 to 4 hours on HIGH.

9. Check the chicken using a meat thermometer. When it reaches 165°F, turn off the slow cooker & let it rest for about 15 to 20 minutes.

10. One thing remains to be done. Remove the chicken & strain the juices to serve over the chicken.

11. Finally carve the chicken & serve.

Serves: 4 to 5

Preparation time: 10 to 15 minutes

Cooking time: 4 hours on HIGH

We all are legends in some ways.

Nutritional information:

Protein 24.9 g

Carbs 10.7 g

Calories 210

Fat 11.4 g

Unique Vegetable and Beef Soup Recipe

A little work here but will be worth it.

Ingredients:

- 32 ounces mixed vegetables (Frozen)
- Seasoning (salt and pepper)
- 1 pound ground beef (Cooked)
- About 2.5 teaspoons dried minced onion
- 103/4 ounces condensed cream of mushroom, undiluted
- 1 can tomato juice (46 ounces)

Directions:

1. First of all, please make sure you've all the ingredients available. Now quickly mix all the ingredients, except the seasoning, in a small or medium bowl.

2. Then pour everything into your slow cooker & cook properly on LOW for about 4 to 5 hours.

3. One thing remains to be done. Season to taste.

4. Finally transfer to a bowl & serve.

Serves: 6 to 7 Prep.

Time: 20 to 25 minutes

Cooking Time: 6 hours

Nutritional information:

Sodium 55 mg

Total Fat 2 g

Protein 6 g

Calories 110

Carbs 18 g

Try it...

Yummy Tomato Hamburger Soup

This is different, isn't it?

Ingredients:

- 1 can V-8 juice
- About 2.5 teaspoon dried onion powder
- 2 packages frozen vegetable mix
- 1 can condensed mushroom soup
- 1-pound ground beef

Directions:

1. First of all, please make sure you've all the ingredients available. In a skillet over medium flame, sauté the ground beef until lightly brown.
2. Now transfer to a crockpot.
3. Place all ingredients in the crockpot.
4. Season with salt & pepper to taste.
5. One thing remains to be done. Then give a good stir to combine everything.

6.   Finally close the lid & cook properly on low for about 7 to 8 hours.

Serves: 8 to 9

Preparation Time: 10 to 15 minutes

Cooking Time: 8 hours

Yeah, this is a new variation.

Nutritional information:

Protein: 18.1g

Fiber: 3.2g

Carbohydrates: 14.8g

Calories per serving: 227

Fat: 10.2g

Tasty Butternut Squash Soup Recipe

Classic, isn't it?

Ingredients:

- 1/2 white onion (Chopped)
- Salt and pepper, to taste
- 5 cloves garlic (Chopped)
- 5 cups vegetable stock (or more, enough to cover squash)
- About 1.5 butternut squash, peeled, cubed

Directions:

1. First of all, please make sure you've all the ingredients available. Then place everything into your crockpot & cook properly on LOW for about 3 to 4 hours.

2. One thing remains to be done. Now quickly transfer the soup to a food

processor or even a blender & purée until smooth.

3.   Finally transfer to a bowl, season with salt and pepper, & serve.

Serves: 8 to 9 Prep.

Time: 10 to 15 minutes

Cooking Time: 4 hours

Nutritional information:

Calories 40

Carbs 2 g

Total Fat 3 g

Sodium 75 mg

Protein 1 g

Different yet fantastic in many ways.

Titanic Home-Style Stew

Yeah, direct from the heaven; yeah?

Ingredients:

- 2 packages frozen vegetables
- A sprig of basil leaves
- 1 can condensed cream of mushroom soup
- 1 can condensed tomato soup
- About 1 1/2 pounds beef stew meat, cut into chunks

Directions:

1. First of all, please make sure you've all the ingredients available. In a skillet over medium flame, sauté the beef until lightly brown.
2. Now transfer to a crockpot.
3. This step is important. Place the mushroom soup, vegetables, & tomato soup in the crockpot.
4. Season with salt & pepper to taste.

5. Then give a good stir to combine everything.
6. One thing remains to be done. Close the lid & cook properly on low for about 7 to 8 hours.
7. Finally garnish with basil leaves.

Serves: 7 to 9

Preparation Time: 10 to 15 minutes

Cooking Time: 8 hours

What's so typical or different here?

Nutritional information:

Protein:30g

Carbohydrates: 41g

Fat: 13g

Fiber: 2g

Calories per serving: 415

Rich Italian Meatball Soup Recipe

Best combo ever... Don't you agree?

Ingredients:

- 2 bags (12 ounces each) Italian-style turkey meatballs, thawed and cooked
- Some fresh oregano (optional)
- 1 can (15 ounces) black beans, rinsed, drained
- 1 bag (10 ounces) frozen soup vegetables
- 1 can (14 ounces) seasoned chicken broth with roasted garlic
- 2 cans (141/2 ounces each) Italian-style tomatoes, diced, undrained

Directions:

1. First of all, please make sure you've all the ingredients available. Mix everything except the oregano in a bowl.

2. Now transfer the mixture to your slow cooker & cook properly on LOW for about 6 to 7 hours.
3. You can also cook properly on HIGH for about 3 to 31/2 hours if you are in a hurry.
4. One thing remains to be done. Then transfer to a bowl & sprinkle with oregano, if desired.
5. Finally serve & enjoy.

Serves: 8 to 9 Prep.

Time: 10 to 15 minutes

Cooking Time: 7 hours

Nutritional information:

Protein 16 g

Calories 288

Sodium 1136 mg

Carbs 33 g

Total Fat 14 g

Someone is definitely ready for this.

Elegant Green Lentil Curry Stew

Good recipe!!

Ingredients:

- 3 cups vegetable broth
- About 1.5 onion (Quartered)
- About 1.5 tablespoon garam masala or curry powder
- 1 can coconut milk
- 2 cans green lentils, drained

Directions:

1. First of all, please make sure you've all the ingredients available. Place all ingredients in the crockpot.
2. Now season with salt & pepper to taste.
3. Give a good stir to combine everything.
4. One thing remains to be done. Then close the lid & cook properly on low for about 3 to 4 hours.

5.　　Finally garnish with chopped cilantro leaves.

Serves: 8 to 9

Preparation Time: 5 to 10 minutes

Cooking Time: 4 hours

Lucky!!

Nutritional information:

Fiber: 2g

Carbohydrates: 13.8g

Fat: 15.4g

Protein: 4.4g

Calories per serving: 196

Wonderful Special Chili Recipe

Yes, this is famous!!

Ingredients:

- 1 can (111/2 ounces) hot-style vegetable juice
- About 1.5 large onion, chopped, cooked with the ground beef
- 1 can (141/2 ounces) tomatoes and green chili, diced, undrained
- 2 15-ounce cans chili beans in chili gravy
- 1 pound ground beef. cooked with the onion

Optional Ingredients:

- Dairy sour cream
- Some green onions
- Cheddar cheese (Shredded)

Directions:

1.   First of all, please make sure you've all the ingredients available. Place all the non-optional ingredients in a slow cooker & cook properly on LOW for about 4 to 6 hours.
2.   Now you can also cook properly on HIGH for about 2 to 3 hours, if in a hurry.
3.   One thing remains to be done. Then garnish with optional ingredients, if desired.
4.   Finally transfer to a bowl & serve.

Serves: 6 to 7 Prep.

Time: 15 to 20 minutes

Cooking Time: 6 hours

Nutritional information:

Protein 23 g

Sodium 873 mg

Carbs 31 g

Total Fat 12 g

Calories 332

Wow, that's cute!!

Quick Creamy Cauliflower Soup

Fresh start with something new!!

Ingredients:

- About 1 cup onions (Chopped)
- 1 cup heavy cream
- 4 cups chicken broth
- 1 tablespoon butter
- 1 cauliflower head (Chopped)

Directions:

1. First of all, please make sure you've all the ingredients available. Place all ingredients in the crockpot.

2. Then season with salt & pepper to taste.

3. Give a good stir to combine everything.

4. One thing remains to be done. Now close the lid & cook properly on low for about 3 to 4 hours.

5. Finally use a hand blender to pulse until smooth.

Try this my way!!

Serves: 4 to 6

Preparation Time: 5 to 10 minutes

Cooking Time: 6 hours

Nutritional information:

Carbohydrates: 7.3g

Fiber: 1.6g

Protein: 53.9g

Fat: 30.8g

Calories per serving: 531

Awesome Special Mexican Soup Recipe

Baking does the trick!!

Ingredients:

- 2 cans (141/2 ounces each) Mexican-style stewed tomatoes
- Shredded Mexican-style or cheddar cheese
- 1 can (103/4 ounces) nacho cheese soup, condensed
- About 1.5 package (10 ounces) whole kernel corn, frozen
- 1 pound chicken breast halves, skinless, boneless, and cut into 1/2-inch cubes

Directions:

1. First of all, please make sure you've all the ingredients available. Now mix all the ingredients except the cheese together in a slow cooker &

cook properly on LOW for about 4 to 5 hours.

2.   One thing remains to be done. You can also cook properly on HIGH for about 2 to 21/2 hours.

3.   Finally transfer to a bowl & garnish with cheese.

Serves: 6 to 7 Prep.

Time: 10 to 15 minutes

Cooking Time: 5 hours

Nutritional information:

Sodium 647 mg

Total Fat 6 g

Carbs 24 g

Calories 224

Protein 23 g

I don't know about you, but I include this one everytime I get a chance.

Legendary Crockpot Lazy Posole

Why not??

Ingredients:

- 1 can white hominy, drained
- Fresh cilantro (Chopped)
- 1 can crushed tomatoes
- 1 packet Mexican seasoning mix
- 1-pound pork tenderloin, cut into chunks

Directions:

1. First of all, please make sure you've all the ingredients available. Place all ingredients in the crockpot except for the cilantro.
2. Now season with salt & pepper to taste.
3. Give a good stir to combine everything.
4. One thing remains to be done. Then close the lid & cook properly on low for about 3 to 4 hours.

5. Finally garnish with chopped cilantro leaves.

Serves: 8 to 9

Preparation Time: 10 to 15 minutes

Cooking Time: 4 hours

Leave a mark!!

Nutritional information:

Fiber: 1.5g

Carbohydrates: 6.7g

Fat: 2.4g

Protein: 15.6g

Calories per serving: 115

Titanic Lamb Curry

Be unique, be extraordinary...

Ingredients:

- 1/2 cup water
- 6 oz fresh baby spinach
- About 5.5 teaspoons curry powder
- 15-ounces marinara sauce, sugar-free
- 1 lb diced lamb

Directions:

1. First of all, please make sure you've all the ingredients available. Place a medium-sized skillet over medium heat, grease with oil & add the diced lamb.

2. Now stir in the curry powder, and a pinch of salt, & cook gently for about 5 to 10 minutes, or until golden brown.

3. This step is important. Transfer the meat into a 4-quart slow-cooker.

4. Stir in the marinara sauce & the water, ensuring the meat is fully immersed in the liquid.

5. Then cover and seal the slow-cooker, allowing the food to cook properly for about 2 to 3 hours at a high heat setting.

6. One thing remains to be done. Stir in the spinach leaves & continue cooking for another half hour, or until the spinach is tender.

7. Finally serve warm with cauliflower rice.

Servings: 4 to 6

Something is special!!

Nutritional information:

Protein: 33 g

Carbohydrates: 5 g

Fats: 17 g

Energy: 310 Kcal

Net Carbs: 4 g

Tasty Sweet and Spicy Lamb

If you're a legend, then make this one.

Ingredients:

- 1 medium-sized white onion, peeled and chopped
- 3/4 cup hot barbecue sauce, low-carb and sugar-free
- About 2.5 garlic cloves (Minced)
- 1 cup sweet and sour sauce, low-carb and sugar-free
- 1/8 teaspoon xanthan gum
- 12 lamb shoulder chops, trimmed and cut into bite-sized pieces

Directions:

1. First of all, please make sure you've all the ingredients available. Grease a 4-

quart slow-cooker with a non-stick cooking spray.

2. Now place the onion, meat pieces, garlic & sauces into the slow-cooker, and cover it with the lid.

3. Allow to cook properly for about 4 to 5 hours at a high heat setting.

4. One thing remains to be done. Then stir in xanthan gum, & continue cooking for about 10 to 15 minutes, until the sauce thickens to the desired consistency.

5. Finally serve warm with cooked cauliflower rice.

Servings: 6 to 7

Being lucky is definitely better.

Nutritional information:

Net Carbs: 0.9 g

Carbohydrates: 0.9 g

Fats: 6.5 g

Energy: 166.3 Kcal

Protein: 23.7 g

Yummy Cinnamon Lamb

Mystery is unveiled!!

Ingredients:

- 4 tomatoes (Chopped)
- 2 cloves of garlic (Minced)
- 1 large bunch of coriander
- About 1.5 tablespoon ground cinnamon
- 2 lb lamb shoulder (Diced)

Directions:

1. First of all, please make sure you've all the ingredients available. Place the lamb in a 4-quart slow-cooker.
2. Now add the tomatoes, cinnamon, garlic, a pinch of salt and pepper, & pour in 1/2 cup water.

3. Cut off the stalks from the coriander bunch & add these.
4. Then cover the slow-cooker with the lid, & set the cooking time for 5 hours, at a low heat setting.
5. One thing remains to be done. After this time, roughly chop the coriander leaves, & add them to the slow-cooker, allowing a further 20 to 25 minutes of cooking time at a high heat setting.
6. Finally serve with cauliflower rice.

Servings: 4 to 6

The speed matters...

Nutritional information:

Protein: 39 g

Carbohydrates: 4 g

Net Carbs: 2.9 g

Fats: 28 g

Energy: 353 Kcal

Unique Lamb Stew

Be super

Ingredients:

- 8 oz turnips and/or carrots, peeled and chopped
- 2 cups beef broth, warmed
- 8 oz mushrooms (Sliced)
- 2 garlic cloves (Minced)
- 8 lamb shoulder chops, trimmed and cut into bite-sized pieces

Directions:

1. First of all, please make sure you've all the ingredients available. Now grease a 4-quarts slow-cooker with a non-stick cooking spray & place all of the

ingredients inside, adding a pinch of salt and pepper.

2. One thing remains to be done. Then cover and seal slow-cooker with its lid, & allow to cook properly for about 5 to 6 hours on a low heat setting.

3. Finally transfer the stew to a serving platter, with all of the cooking juices, garnish with mint leaves, & serve.

Servings: 4 to 6

Deserved!!

Nutritional information:

Protein: 53 g

Carbohydrates: 13 g

Energy: 405 Kcal

Fats: 18.9 g

Net Carbs: 9.7 g

Ultimate Lamb and Green Beans

Long way to go...

Ingredients:

- 6 cups fresh green beans, trimmed
- 2 cups of chicken broth or water
- 4 cloves of garlic, peeled and sliced
- About 2.5 tablespoons dried mint
- 3 lb lamb leg, on the bone

Directions:

1. First of all, please make sure you've all the ingredients available. Now quickly season the lamb on all sides with salt & black pepper.
2. Then place a large skillet over a medium heat, allow 2 tablespoons of

butter to melt, then add the seasoned lamb.

3. Allow to brown, turning frequently, to ensure that it is golden brown on all sides. This should take 10 to 15 minutes.

4. This step is important. Transfer the lamb to the slow-cooker, sprinkle with the garlic and mint, & add the water.

5. Now cover the slow-cooker with the lid, & allow the lamb to cook for about 5 to 6 hours at a high heat setting.

6. Check occasionally and if the lamb gets dry, pour in an additional 1/2 cup of water.

7. One thing remains to be done. Place the beans into the slow-cooker, & allow to continue cooking for another hour. The beans should be tender-crisp.

8. Finally serve hot, although the leftover meat can also be enjoyed cold.

Servings: 4 to 6

Cooking level infinite….

Nutritional information:

Carbohydrates: 14 g

Protein: 37.4 g

Net Carbs: 7.5 g

Fats: 36.5 g

Energy: 525 Kcal

Awesome Lamb Shoulder

Uber fantastic!!

Ingredients:

- 2 tablespoons mixed herbs
- 2 cups chicken stock, warmed
- About 1/2 teaspoon xanthan gum
- 1 lamb shoulder, on the bone

Directions:

1. First of all, please make sure you've all the ingredients available. Grease a 4-quarts slow-cooker with a non-stick cooking spray.
2. Now season the lamb with the mixed herbs & a pinch of salt and pepper, and place it in the slow-cooker.

3. This step is important. Pour over the stock, and seal the slow-cooker with its lid. Set the cooking timer for about 7 to 8 hours, and allow the meat to cook on a low heat setting, or until the meat is tender.

4. Then when the lamb is cooked to your liking, transfer it to a plate & keep warm.

5. One thing remains to be done. Transfer the cooking liquid into a saucepan, stir in the xanthan gum & allow to cook gently until the gravy has reduced to the desired thickness.

6. Finally carve the meat into slices, & serve with a jug of gravy alongside.

Servings: 4 to 5

For those who are not ordinary, try this one.

Nutritional information:

Protein: 39 g

Net Carbs: 1 g

Fats: 36 g

Carbohydrates: 1 g

Energy: 488 Kcal

Super Chinese Style Lamb Shoulder

Be amazed ?

Ingredients:

- 5 carrots, peeled and cut into chunks
- About 2.5 teaspoons Chinese five spice powder, and 2 tablespoons soy sauce
- 1 large white onion, peeled and chopped
- 3 lb lamb shoulder
- 1/4 cup minced ginger

Directions:

1. First of all, please make sure you've all the ingredients available. Place the

ginger, onion, & carrots in a 4-quart slow-cooker.

2. Now mix the soy sauce & the Chinese 5 spice powder together, then rub this mixture over the lamb shoulder.

3. Now please place the lamb on top of the vegetables in the slow-cooker & then place the lid on the slow-cooker.

4. One thing remains to be done. Then allow to cook properly for about 3 to 4 hours at a high heat setting.

5. Finally serve the cooked vegetables alongside the lamb.

Servings: 4 to 5

Wow, just wow!!

Nutritional information:

Protein: 44 g

Carbohydrates: 5 g

Energy: 412.8 Kcal

Fats: 20.9 g

Net Carbs: 4.7 g

Delightful Lamb with Edamame Beans and Tomatoes

Show time!!

Ingredients:

- 1 cup frozen edamame beans, thawed
- About 2.5 teaspoons curry powder,
- 3 cups diced tomatoes,
- About 1.5 tablespoon minced garlic
- 12 oz ground lamb

Directions:

1. First of all, please make sure you've all the ingredients available. Grease a 4-quarts slow-cooker with a non-stick cooking spray & place all of the ingredients inside.

2. Now season with salt to taste, then stir in 1 1/2 cups of water.
3. One thing remains to be done. Cover the slow-cooker with its lid, & allow the food to cook for about 5 to 6 hours at a low heat setting.
4. Finally pour into warmed bowls, & serve immediately.

Servings: 8 to 9

Feast for you!!

Nutritional information:

Carbohydrates: 13.8 g

Protein: 38.4 g

Energy: 243.4 Kcal

Fats: 15.4 g

Net Carbs: 9.6 g

Fantastic Mustard Lamb

Being super is a matter of recipe... ?

Ingredients:

- 1/4 cup Dijon mustard
- 1/2 cup chicken stock
- 1 cup raw honey
- 12 lamb shoulder chops, trimmed

Directions:

1. First of all, please make sure you've all the ingredients available. Grease a 4-quarts slow-cooker with a non-stick cooking spray & place the lamb chops inside.

2. Now stir the remaining ingredients together in a bowl, until mixed well, & pour this mixture over the lamb chops.

3. One thing remains to be done. Cover the slow-cooker with its lid, and set the cooking timer for about 4 to 5 hours, allowing to cook properly at a high heat setting.
4. Finally serve immediately.

Servings: 6 to 7

Being a legend.

Nutritional information:

Protein: 26 g

Energy: 153 Kcal

Carbohydrates: 2 g

Fats: 4 g

Net Carbs: 2 g

Great Lamb with Onions and Thyme

When you're fantastic, this is best!!

Ingredients:

- 4 large white onions, peeled and diced
- 10 fl oz red wine
- small bunch thyme sprigs
- 1/2 cup parsley leaves
- 6 lb leg of lamb

Directions:

1. First of all, please make sure you've all the ingredients available. Season the leg of lamb with a pinch of salt and black pepper.
2. Now place a large skillet over a medium heat, & add 2 tablespoons of oil.

3. Allow the lamb to turn golden-brown on all sides, turning frequently for about 15 to 20 minutes.
4. This step is important. Transfer the lamb onto a plate & add the onions into the pan.
5. Then allow to cook gently for about 10 to 15 minutes, until the onions are soft & lightly browned.
6. Spoon onion mixture into a 4-quart slow-cooker, then add the lamb, the wine, and the herbs.
7. One thing remains to be done. Seal the slow-cooker with its lid, & allow to cook properly on a high heat for about 3 to 4 hours.
8. Finally garnish with thyme sprigs to serve.

Servings: 4 to 6

Being rich is a plus point ?

Nutritional information:

Protein: 19 g

Carbohydrates: 3 g

Net Carbs: 2.6 g

Fats: 12 g

Energy: 183 Kcal

Thanks for reading my book.

Made in the USA
Las Vegas, NV
25 June 2022